D0383020

URBAN LEGENDS

CREATURES

C.M. Johnson

Creatures

Origins: Urban Legends

Copyright © 2018
Published by Full Tilt Press
Written by C.M. Johnson
All rights reserved.

Printed in the United States of America.
No part of this book may be reproduced in any manner whatsoever without written permission,
except in the case of brief quotations embodied in critical articles and reviews.

Full Tilt Press
42982 Osgood Road
Fremont, CA 94539

Full Tilt Press publications may be purchased for educational, business, or sales promotional use.

Editorial Credits
Design and layout by Sara Radka
Edited by Lauren Dupuis-Perez
Copyedited by Renae Gilles

Image Credits
Getty Images: iStockphoto, cover, 4, 8, 11, 14, 18, 20, 24, 25, 28, 33, 34, 37, 38; Newscom: Alan Berner/KRT, 10, Duncan Williams/Cal Sport Media, 43, KRT, 12, Polaris, 13; Shutterstock: anthony heflin, 15, 17, Creative Lab, 7, Denis Belitsky, 44, Eric Isselee, 35, Everett Historical, 41, johnnychaos, 40, karamysh, 26, Leszek Kobusinski, 21, Mark Caunt, 36, okhanchikov, 27, randy andy, 6, Ricardo Reitmeyer, 23, romakoma, 30, Roman Pyshchyk, 32, Teri Virbickis, 5, UnderTheSea, 31, Zacarias Pereira da Mata, 16; Vecteezy: 46, background and cover elements

ISBN: 978-1-62920-608-0 (library binding)
ISBN: 978-1-62920-620-2 (eBook)

Contents

LIBRARY
DEXTER SCHOOLS
DEXTER, NM 88230

SASQUATCH

If the sasquatch exists, it most likely lives in thick forests.

INTRODUCTION

Campers hear grunts in the darkness. Hunters come face-to-face with a hairy, human-like creature. It walks on two feet. It is over 7 feet (200 centimeters) tall. The campers' dogs run in terror.

For hundreds of years, people have reported seeing a sasquatch, or bigfoot, in the woods. Most sightings occur in the United States' Pacific Northwest region and in Canada. Reports have also been made in other rural parts of the United States. The sasquatch looks like a cross between a human and an ape. It is covered in black, brown, red, or gray hair. Its feet range from 15 to more than 20 inches (38 to 51 centimeters) long. It weighs 500 to 1,000 pounds (227 to 454 kilograms). Another name for the sasquatch is "skunk ape." This name comes from its bad smell. People say the odor is like breathing through a dirty diaper.

Many people have said they've seen a bigfoot near Pikes Peak in Colorado.

DID YOU KNOW?
One of the earliest accounts of a sasquatch was written in 1792 by Spanish explorer José Mariano Moziño.

Some footprints and photos of the sasquatch have turned out to be fake. Other witnesses are sure that what they saw was real.

One of the most famous sasquatch sightings was near California's Bluff Creek Historical Trail.

BEST RECORDED SIGHTING

It was 1967. Roger Patterson and Bob Gimlin were exploring in California, near Bluff Creek. Something spooked their horses. Patterson filmed what looks like a female sasquatch. In the film, she has big muscles. Her long arms swing back and forth. She turns to look at the men, then disappears into the trees.

Experts looked at the film. John Napier, a biologist, saw a creature that looked like it was half-human, half-ape. Grover Krantz, an **anthropologist**, thought the creature was an unknown type of **primate**.

anthropologist: a person who studies human societies and cultures

primate: a group of mammals that includes humans, apes, monkeys, tarsiers, lemurs, and lorises

Patterson had been looking for a sasquatch for a long time. He loved the idea of proving that the creatures were real. Excitement about the film helped him raise money for more searches.

DID YOU KNOW?
You can see the famous video for yourself by searching for "Patterson-Gimlin Film" on YouTube.

More than 30 years later, a man named Bill Heironimus came forward. He claimed that the film was a hoax. He said he was paid by Patterson to dress up as the bigfoot. Another man supported that claim. He said he'd sold Patterson a gorilla suit. But Patterson always said he was telling the truth. The film is now online, and people still study it today.

In 1972, Bob Gimlin visited Patterson, who was sick with cancer. Patterson said that when he got better, he wanted to go back to Bluff Creek with Gimlin. He told his friend that, this time, they would finally catch a sasquatch. Sadly, Patterson died the next day.

Experts are still not sure if the figure in Roger Patterson's video was a man in a gorilla costume pretending to be a sasquach.

TIMELINE

Sightings of the sasquatch began long ago and continue today.

Pre-1800s

Most Native North American peoples have a word for "wild man."

1811

David Thompson finds a footprint in the mountains of Alberta, Canada. It is 14 inches (36 cm) long and 8 inches (20 cm) wide.

1924

Near Vancouver, British Columbia, Albert Ostman is reportedly held captive by a sasquatch family. After a week, he escapes.

1930

Berry-pickers near Mount St. Helens, in Washington state, find huge footprints.

1972

Al Berry records the creepy sounds of grunts and whistles. He is in the Sierra Nevada mountains, in California. This recording is known as the "Sierra Sounds." Berry thinks it is a group of sasquatches.

1969

Frank Hansen finds a "man-ape" encased in ice at a Minnesota farm. He calls it an "Iceman."

2009

A Georgia police officer sees a large animal walking upright across the road. His dashcam records a video of the creature.

1967

Roger Patterson films a sasquatch near Bluff Creek.

2012

Investigators in Florida take a video that records body heat. The "heat image" looks like a bigfoot.

EVIDENCE FOR AND AGAINST

It is often hard to tell whether a sasquatch story is real or not.

Rant Mullens was a retired logger. In 1982, he confessed to carving a pair of big feet out of wood. He used these feet to create the tracks near the Mount St. Helens berry patch. Ray Wallace also built fake "feet" to create sasquatch tracks near Bluff Creek. After Wallace died, his family came forward with the truth.

It is easy to doubt people who profit from their "proof." Frank Hansen showed off his "Iceman" at carnivals. However, he let scientists look at it only through the ice. He never let anyone thaw it or do any tests.

Bigfoot investigators often make plaster casts of footprints for experts to study.

Yeti

The yeti is a sasquatch-like creature. It is said to live in the snowy peaks of the Himalaya Mountains. Unlike its brown-haired cousin, the yeti is said to be covered in white hair. This helps it hide in the snow. In February of 2016, a skier filmed a mysterious creature in a Spanish mountain resort town. The video clearly shows a large white figure walking among the snow-covered trees. Could this be a real yeti?

Eyewitness accounts are the hardest to confirm or deny. For more than 30 years, Albert Ostman kept the story of his 1924 abduction a secret. He was afraid people would think he was crazy. But many people do believe that his story is true.

Some sasquatch evidence is very convincing. Scott Nelson is a **crypto-linguist** who worked in the U.S. Navy. Nelson says the grunts and hoots on the "Sierra Sounds" recordings make up a real language. But no one knows what the sounds could mean.

crypto-linguist: someone responsible for identifying foreign communications

Until his death in 2016, Charles DeVore of the Texas Bigfoot Research Center investigated many reported sasquatch sightings in east Texas.

Is It Out There?

The sasquatch is unknown to science. No one has ever captured one, or even found a body or a bone. Does that mean the creatures don't exist?

Writers like Tom Burnette say sasquatches might be too smart for us. They might bury their dead and avoid being seen. Maybe this is why sasquatches seem to hate dogs. Dogs might be able to easily smell and track the creatures. People rarely report sasquatches being aggressive toward humans. But some have said their dogs were attacked.

Some scientists don't think an animal as big as a sasquatch could survive. There aren't many food sources in North American forests. Jane Goodall is a chimpanzee expert. She says that the sasquatch probably does exist. Killing a bigfoot is even banned in some places, such as Skamania County in Washington state. Anyone who kills a bigfoot might pay a fine or even go to jail.

Many reports of a sasquatch turn out to be hoaxes. But one faked report doesn't mean another isn't real. Every day, people still head out into the woods. They keep their eyes and ears open. Maybe, they will be the one to find a sasquatch.

DID YOU KNOW?
Every year, 15,000 to 20,000 new species of plants, animals, and insects are discovered.

Ray Wallace of Toledo, Washington, made several plaster casts of what he said were sasquatch footprints.

SNALLYGASTER

People have described the snallygaster as being a cross between a bird and a reptile.

INTRODUCTION

The snallygaster is not shy. This dragon-like monster spies its prey with only one red eye in the middle of its forehead. It shrieks like a train and swoops down low. Legends say that it snatches up chickens and children.

Stories about the snallygaster began in the 1700s. German immigrants lived near the Blue Ridge mountains in rural Maryland. They spoke of a creature called the *schneller geist*. This is where the word "snallygaster" came from. *Schneller geist* means "quick spirit."

In 1909, Maryland newspapers wrote about the creature. They talked about its "reign of terror." It was seen most often in Frederick and Washington counties. After a few months, the animal finally seemed to disappear. But in 1932, people reported seeing it again.

DID YOU KNOW?
The first known German settlers in the Maryland area arrived in 1681. Just 20 years later, tales of the snallygaster began to spread.

The Blue Ridge mountain range extends 615 miles (990 kilometers) from Pennsylvania to Georgia.

It is said that the snallygaster hunts mostly at night.

BEST RECORDED SIGHTING

In Feburary of 1909, James Harding said he saw a snallygaster in the sky. Soon, more and more people saw it. Most sightings were in Maryland, but reports also came in from nearby states.

Newspapers said the snallygaster snatched up a man named Bill Gifferson. The papers said the snallygaster pierced his neck, drank his blood, then dropped him down a hill.

The legends said that the snallygaster laid eggs as big as barrels. The stories say that some men built a huge **incubator** to hatch the eggs.

incubator: a device used to hatch eggs in a controlled environment

President Teddy Roosevelt heard the reports. He liked to hunt big **game**. The paper said he might cancel a trip to Africa. He wanted to find the snallygaster. But the snallygaster hunt did not happen. In March of 1909, three men said they fought the beast and chased it into the woods. After that, there were no more encounters for years.

In 1932, reports of the snallygaster returned. Had this beast hatched from a 1909 egg? The stories say that this new snallygaster flew over a large vat of moonshine. It fell into the boiling **mash**. The dead creature was found by **federal agents**, who were looking for illegal moonshine. They blew up both the still and the snallygaster.

game: wild animals hunted for sport or food

mash: a mixture of powdered malt and hot water used in brewing

federal agent: a detective or investigator who works for a national government

Between 1920 and 1933, it was illegal to make or sell alcohol in the United States. But many people used a still to make their own.

TIMELINE

Sightings of the snallygaster have been reported for more than 100 years.

1909

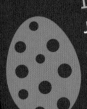

James Harding sees the snallygaster.

The monster kills Bill Gifferson.

The snallygaster lays an egg near Sharpsburg, Maryland. It lays a second near Burkittsville.

1909

Three men say they fight the creature in Frederick County. The fight lasts an hour and a half. Reports of the beast stop.

1932

Two men spot a snallygaster.

1932

The snallygaster flies over a vat of moonshine in Frog Hollow, Maryland. The beast dies in the vat. Its body is destroyed by federal agents.

1973

In Baltimore County, Maryland, people say a snallygaster is hunting cows.

1946

A hunter in Doddridge County, West Virginia, speaks up. He says he has found a snallygaster "cub."

1976

The *Washington Post* funds a search for the snallygaster.

1935–1941

A snallygaster is seen in West Virginia. It chases a man named Kennie Bland up a tree. It paralyzes a hound called Old Dog Blue.

2014

In Preston County, West Virginia, a man says he saw a snallygaster. He shows photos to prove it. The cast of the TV show *Mountain Monsters* go on a hunt for it. They come up empty-handed.

Dragons are common in German myths and stories.

Evidence For and Against

In 1909, two Maryland newspapers wrote about the snallygaster. The newspaper with the most details on the beast would win the most readers. But the reports sounded like "tall tales." Each snallygaster was fiercer or weirder than the one before. In 1909, the stories said that a snallygaster told a man it was thirsty and wanted a drink. In 1932, the beast rode a flying bicycle and wore water wings.

Maybe the stories were made up for other reasons. The towns where the snallygaster was seen were close to a busy road. The motor car was a recent invention, and traffic was getting heavier. Did locals want to scare away outsiders? Legends of a monster might keep unwanted strangers away.

However, back in the 1700s, some people were truly scared of the snallygaster. They painted special charms on their houses and barns to keep the monster away. Today, reports are still made of a beast in the sky. People claim that this predator kills cows and dogs.

Early immigrants often nailed a horseshoe over their doors. It was thought to bring good luck and to keep evil away.

Motor Cars

In 1913, there were only 606,124 motor cars in the world. The United States made about 485,000 of them. By 1927, about 15 million Ford Model T cars had been sold. The motor vehicle industry was booming. As more people started driving motor cars, modern roads became more common. Rural communities became easier to access. The population of the United States began to move more freely between cities and towns.

Is It Out There?

Could other animals be mistaken for the snallygaster? Tim Iverson is a **naturalist** from Maryland. He says that the common barn owl has some "monster credentials." This owl has a loud shriek. It bobs its head from side to side. It has a very large wingspan, black eyes, and a fierce beak. It can attack its prey in total darkness.

DID YOU KNOW?
Using frightening legends to scare children is common around the world. In Japan, the demonlike *namahage* visit families on New Year's to ask if there are any misbehaving children.

In 1932, the *Baltimore Sun* reported the snallygaster's death. They printed a photo of what they said was the dead monster. The image is not clear, and recent photos of the beast are also blurry. No one has ever come forward with a body or an egg.

Whether or not the snallygaster is real, parents find the legends useful. Parents warn their children not to stray too far from the house. If you go too far or stay out too late, you might run into the beast . . .

naturalist: an expert on the history of animals and plants

Owls can sneak up on their prey thanks to their special wings, which allow them to fly silently.

OGOPOGO

Ogopogo is the most-sighted lake monster in the world. Each year there are up to 10 reported sightings.

INTRODUCTION

Hundreds of years ago, Native Canadians feared a "demon" in Lake Okanagan. This lake is located in British Columbia, Canada. Today, people still claim to see a monster in the lake. This creature has been named "Ogopogo." It has been spotted more times than the Loch Ness monster.

Ogopogo is slim and snakelike. It has a head like a horse or a goat. It is between 15 and 50 feet (5 and 15 meters) long. Its skin is dark and smooth. It lives in the **depths** or in caves along the shore, and it comes to the surface to eat fish. Swimmers say they have been chased by the giant beast.

Videos show what could be a creature with humps or coils moving in and out of the water. Some scientists say the pictures show logs or waves. Others see known animals, such as beavers. But some people think the legend could be true. They search for proof of Ogopogo.

It is said that Ogopogo lives in an underwater cave off Squally Point, near Lake Okanagan's Rattlesnake Island.

DID YOU KNOW?
The earliest record of the Loch Ness monster appeared in a biography of Saint Columba, written in AD 565.

depths: an area far below the surface of the water

Lake Okanagan is 84 miles (135 km) long.

BEST RECORDED SIGHTING

Thousands of people have said they've seen Ogopogo. In 1968, a man named Arthur Folden was one of them. He also said he had proof. Folden had seen something alive out on the lake. He had taken out a home-movie camera and filmed the unknown creature.

The August day was sunny and the water was calm. Folden's film is dark and grainy. But it is clear that something disturbs the water. It moves to the right of the screen. It starts moving quickly. Whatever it is, it leaves a long wake.

Some people say the film shows a big animal. They compare its long length to the trees along the shore. They say its head and tail are a long ways apart. Each end breaks the surface of the water at the same time.

In 2005, National Geographic asked Benjamin Radford, a scientist, to look at the film. Radford and other scientists did visual experiments. Radford decided the subject of the film was indeed alive, but he thought it was a bird or a beaver. He said Folden was too far away to clearly see the size of the creature.

DID YOU KNOW?
It is hard to know for sure how many beavers live around Lake Okanagan because they are most active at night and roam large areas of land.

Could small animals or birds really make such big splashes in the lake?

TIMELINE

People have been reporting Ogopogo stalking the waters of Lake Okanagan for hundreds of years.

Pre-1800s

Native Canadians draw "N'ha-a-itk" on stones. Warriors test their bravery with a swim to Rattlesnake Island. The beast is said to live near it.

1914

Locals find the body of an unknown animal on the shore of Lake Okanagan. A naturalist says it is a manatee. But manatees live only in warm places. Is this a baby Ogopogo?

1924

The name "Ogopogo" is given to the creature in the lake. The name might have come from the newly popular pogo stick.

1949

A group on a boat sees an odd animal. It is 30 feet (9 m) long. It has a forked tail.

1968

Arthur Folden films an unknown creature.

2000

Daryl Ellis swims the lake. Ellis sees two long, dark creatures. They swim with him for two hours.

1926

Thirty carloads of people say they see the beast. They watch it at the same time.

2011

Richard Huls films a long shape in the water.

Evidence For and Against

In 2014, Benjamin Radford looked at Richard Huls's video. While Huls saw one long shape, Radford thought he saw two short, straight ones. They seemed to float at different angles. Radford decided they were logs. Timber companies work on Lake Okanagan. Thousands of logs float in the water. These logs could have been mistaken for a creature.

Many people who report seeing Ogopogo say it looked like a log that came alive.

What about the stories of eyewitnesses? The descriptions are usually similar. People see a slim neck and a dark color. They see a creature bigger than any fish. They say a "serpent" coils through the lake. It chases their boats. Its large head bursts out of the water.

The number of sightings is very high. In 1926, the editor of the *Vancouver Sun* made a case for Ogopogo. He said too many people had seen a beast in the lake. Could they all be wrong? Today, **cryptozoologist** John Kirk agrees. Kirk doubts the existence of the Loch Ness monster, but he says he's seen Ogopogo himself.

cryptozoologist: a person who studies creatures from myth and legend

Cave Creatures

Many different kinds of creatures live in caves. Some cave species are so rare, they can be found in only one single cave. Olms are one type of rare cave creature. They have no eyes, are completely white, and look like dragons. They can grow to be up to 1 foot (30 cm) long. Olms are a kind of amphibian, like a salamander. They can be found in the water caves of Slovenia and Croatia.

Researchers went on a search in 2008. Divers found large sinkholes on the bottom of the lake. Some water creatures burrow in the sand. They do this to hide from predators. Others hide and then surprise their prey. Could Ogopogo be hiding there?

Investigators have used divers and even submarines to search for Ogopogo.

The sturgeon's whiskers are called "barbels." They help it find snails and clams that live at the bottom of the lake.

Is It Out There?

If Ogopogo is not a beaver, a bird, or a log, what is it? Some scientists think it could be a fish called a sturgeon. Sturgeons are grayish-green. They have pointed snouts and whisker-like features. This is similar to how people have described Ogopogo. Sturgeons live a long time. In 1953, one was caught in a Canadian lake. It was 152 years old, and it was more than 6 feet (1.8 m) long.

elderly: old

prehistoric: from a time before recorded history

But some people think even an **elderly** sturgeon is too small to be Ogopogo. Some think the beast is a dinosaur. Others say it might be a **prehistoric** whale.

New species are still being found in the ocean. Could a new species of whale remain hidden in a lake? Lake Okanagan is very deep. It has many big caves that are hard to explore.

DID YOU KNOW?
Lake Okanagan has more than 30 beaches, many of which are hard to get to.

Human beings are land creatures. It is exciting to imagine monsters living in places we cannot see. The sun sparkles on beautiful Lake Okanagan. It reflects pine trees and mountains. Could hope and fear make shadows in the lake look bigger than they are? Or could there really be a mysterious creature living in the depths?

LIBRARY
DEXTER SCHOOLS
DEXTER, NM 88230

If there is an unknown creature in Lake Okanagan, is it as fierce as early native people and settlers said it was?

JERSEY DEVIL

The Jersey devil is said to live in the Pine Barrens, a remote place with thick forests and swamps.

INTRODUCTION

Even among strange creatures, the Jersey devil stands out. Legends say it has the head of a horse and the face of a dog. Its wings are leathery, like a bat's. It stands on two powerful legs. It has hooves like a goat, and its tail is long and forked. The creature hisses and shrieks. It attacks small animals. Its appearance is sometimes seen as a sign of imminent disaster.

The legends claim that the Jersey devil was born in 1735, in southern New Jersey. A woman named Mother Leeds was pregnant with her 13th child, but she had decided that 12 was enough. She said the devil could take it. When the baby was born, it sprouted wings. It flew up the chimney and escaped into the wilds of New Jersey. According to eyewitnesses, it didn't stay there.

The Jersey devil, like the figure of Satan in folklore, has some of the features of a goat.

DID YOU KNOW?

During the 1700s, in the North American colonies, women gave birth to an average of eight children.

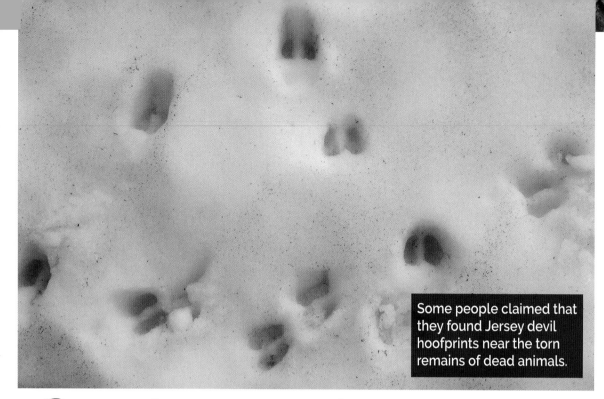

Some people claimed that they found Jersey devil hoofprints near the torn remains of dead animals.

Best Recorded Sighting

According to legend, the Jersey devil appeared a few times in the 1700s and 1800s. In January of 1909, it made its most famous appearances.

One morning, residents woke to find hoofprints on their lawns and on rooftops. Many trails just stopped. Had the animal flown away? On January 16, E.W. Minister saw a glowing creature in the sky. A police officer said he saw it the same night. He shot at it. The beast flew off.

DID YOU KNOW?
Many legendary creatures have wings. Pegasus is a winged horse from Greek mythology. He is pure white.

On January 19, a couple in Gloucester City had a lengthy sighting. A terrible sound woke them. There was an ugly winged creature standing on the roof of their shed. The man put his head out the window. He yelled, "Shoo!" The creature barked at him. Then it left.

The next day, a newspaper printed the story of the couple's encounter. An artist drew a sketch. The story and image created a panic. People were afraid to go outside. The papers reported sightings in several towns. The beast was said to have attacked a dog. It flew at a trolley. It left the remains of devoured animals in the snow.

Drawings of the Jersey devil showed a frightening creature.

TIMELINE

The story of the Jersey devil started long ago and continues to be told today.

1740
According to legend, a minister tries to exorcize the creature.

1735
The legend of the Jersey devil is born.

1800
Commodore Stephen Decatur says he spotted the Jersey devil and shot at it, but it escaped.

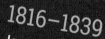

1816–1839
Joseph Bonaparte, Napoleon's brother, goes hunting in the Pine Barrens. He tells people that he saw the Jersey devil.

1960

Bizarre cries terrify people near Mays Landing, in New Jersey. The sounds are never explained.

1993

A forest ranger is driving along the Mullica River in southern New Jersey. He says the Jersey devil blocked the road.

January 16–23, 1909

Thousands of people report sightings. Many parents keep their children home from school. Some schools and businesses close due to panic.

2015

Dave Black takes a photo of a brown, winged creature. He claims it is the Jersey devil.

The Leeds family owned land in the Pine Barrens since the 1690s.

EVIDENCE FOR AND AGAINST

The story of the Jersey devil has many twists. Some events were written down. Others are legends. There seems to be no record of them.

Brian Regal, a historian, studied the papers of early New Jersey. He did not find any stories about Mother Leeds. No one talks about a devil child. The Jersey devil is not blamed for any dead animals. In fact, the legend does not show up until the 1900s. Were its colonial roots made up?

Regal says they were. He also says Benjamin Franklin might have added to the legends. Franklin printed almanacs. So did the Leeds family. In the 1730s, Franklin began to make fun of the Leeds. The Leeds were interested in astrology. They studied demons. Those facts were already hurting the Leeds's business. Franklin joked that writer Titan Leeds was a ghost. He helped to give the Leeds a bad reputation.

The Leeds family crest has winged figures on it. The wings look like a bat's. The figures have claws. They have long tails. The Leeds were from the Pine Barrens. Are these the details that created the legend of the Jersey devil?

Benjamin Franklin

Benjamin Franklin played a major part in the American Revolution (1775–1783). He was also a scientist, a writer, and a diplomat. As a scientist he is best known for doing experiments with electricity. As a writer, Benjamin Franklin is best known for writing his autobiography and *Poor Richard's Almanack*. The *Almanack* included a calendar, weather predictions, poems, jokes, and astronomy. Sometimes it also featured math questions. One piece in the *Almanack*, an essay called "The Way to Wealth," was reprinted in Europe and even translated into French.

Is It Out There?

The story of the Leeds's demon baby might have been a mean joke. But what do we really know about the events of 1909?

Newspapers make it clear that residents were truly frightened. Schools were closed. Could the monster have been faked? Ken Gerhard suspects it was. Gerhard is a writer and cryptozoologist. He says it could have been a trick. Maybe someone wanted to buy cheap land. Homeowners who found strange hoofprints might want to move somewhere else, fast.

DID YOU KNOW?
New Jersey's National Hockey League team is called the New Jersey Devils.

Or maybe someone had another **con** in mind. At one point during the crisis, two men came forward. They said they had caught the beast. People could pay to see it. But it turned out to be a kangaroo. It had been painted. Wings had been glued to its back.

The figures in recent videos and photos of "Jersey devils" look stiff. The creatures look stuffed.

Some local residents say the newspaper reports and hoaxes are one thing. But hearing their grandparents' stories of what they met, at dusk, in the remote, thick forests of the Barrens? That is quite another.

con: a dishonest trick

The New Jersey Devils' mascot skates on the ice at hockey games.

CONCLUSION

Maybe there are things in this world that want to stay hidden. Creatures that lurk in the shadows. Creatures from a time long ago. Maybe they don't belong in this modern world. Did the growing population in the Northeast push out the Jersey devil? Was the snallygaster nothing more than a story to scare away tourists? Are Ogopogo and the Loch Ness monster cousins? Do sasquatch roam the forests of North America?

The excitement of an urban legend is that no one really knows the truth. But that doesn't stop the story. There are still believers. Do these creatures really exist in the dark part of the forest? In the deep parts of the lake? Or do they exist only because we believe they do?

GLOSSARY

anthropologist: a person who studies human societies and cultures

con: a dishonest trick

crypto-linguist: someone responsible for identifying foreign communications

cryptozoologist: a person who studies creatures from myth and legend

depths: an area far below the surface of the water

elderly: old

federal agent: a detective or investigator who works for a national government

game: wild animals hunted for sport or food

incubator: a device used to hatch eggs in a controlled environment

mash: a mixture of powdered malt and hot water used in brewing

naturalist: an expert on the history of animals and plants

prehistoric: from a time before recorded history

primate: a group of mammals that includes humans, apes, monkeys, tarsiers, lemurs, and lorises

Quiz

In what region are most sightings of the sasquatch?

Answer: The Pacific Northwest

Which year did the Patterson-Gimlin Film come out?

Answer: 1967

Who reported the first sightings of the snallygaster?

Answer: Maryland newspapers

What year was the Ogopogo given its name?

Answer: 1924

In 1909, reports of hoofprints were found on people's lawns and where else?

Answer: Their rooftops

In 1932, who found the dead snallygaster?

Answer: Federal agents

INDEX

SELECTED BIBLIOGRAPHY

Costello, Peter. *In Search of Lake Monsters.* New York, NY: Coward, McCann & Geoghegan, 1974.

Fair, Susan. "Mountain Monster: The Snallygaster." *Blue Ridge Country.* January 1, 2012. Web. Accessed February 6, 2017. http://blueridgecountry.com/archive/favorites/snallygaster-monster/.

Gerhard, Ken. *Encounters with Flying Humanoids: Mothman, Manbirds, Gargoyles, & Other Winged Beasts.* Woodbury, MN: Llewellyn Publications, 2013.

Napier, John. *Bigfoot: The Yeti and Sasquatch in Myth and Reality.* New York, NY: E.P. Dutton & Co., Inc., 1973.

Nickell, Joe. *Tracking the Man-Beasts: Sasquatch, Vampires, Zombies, and More.* Amherst, NY: Prometheus Books, 2011.

Radford, Benjamin. "Ogopogo: Canada's Loch Ness Monster." *Live Science.* January 7, 2014. Web. Accessed February 6, 2017. http://www.livescience.com/42399-ogopogo.html.

Storm, Rory. *Monster Hunt: The Guide to Cryptozoology.* New York, NY: Sterling Publishing Co., Inc., 2008.

"Patterson – Gimlin Bigfoot Footage." *Animal Planet.* Web. Accessed February 6, 2017. http://www.animalplanet.com/tv-shows/finding-bigfoot/videos/patterson-gimlin-bigfoot-footage/.